Encyclopedia Brown's Record Book Of Weird And Wonderful Facts

Elkhart Community Schools

Chapter I Program

BROOKDALE

OTHER YEARLING BOOKS YOU WILL ENJOY:

Encyclopedia Brown's Record Book Of Weird And Wonderful Facts

By Donald J. Sobol

Illustrated by
Sal Murdocca

A YEARLING BOOK

Published by
Dell Publishing Co., Inc.
1 Dag Hammarskjold Plaza
New York, New York 10017

Yearling ® TM 913705, Dell Publishing Co., Inc.

ISBN: 0-440-42361-9

Reprinted by arrangement with Delacorte Press
Printed in the United States of America
Third Dell printing—October 1981
CW

For Margot S. Berman

Acknowledgments

For help in the preparation of this book, I wish to thank Don W. Carter of Fortuna, California; Louis P. Daniels of Monroe, Wisconsin; Cindy Day of Melvern, Kansas; James A. Edris of Hershey, Pennsylvania; Joe Gendron of Pomona, California; William Glover of New York, New York; R. Keith Green of Sante Fe, New Mexico; Robert Hunter of Dallas, Oregon; Sam Jesky of Florence, Wisconsin; Ellen D. Langill of Hartland, Wisconsin; Donna LeVie of Fort Lauderdale, Florida; Sandra McDonough of Portland, Oregon; Eleanor Morey of Harrison, New York; Al Powell, Kurt Severin, and Dennis Wepman of Miami, Florida; Steve Reller of Columbia, Missouri; Barbara Sobol of Ridgefield, Connecticut; and Robert W. Wright of Anchorage, Alaska.

—D.J.S.

Contents

Encyclopedia Brown's Record Book Of Weird And Wonderful Facts

Flabbergasting Facts

All the people in the world would fit easily into a box a mile high by a mile wide by a mile long, and the box would fit easily into the Grand Canyon.

In a normal workday a typist's fingers travel 12.6 miles.

In 1977 the United States government spent $1 billion a day. That comes to 53 tons of $20 bills, or as much as the weight of about 50 subcompact cars.

If you're still having difficulty grasping a billion, think of it this way:

One billion minutes ago Jesus still walked the earth.

In 1921 immigrants on Ellis Island, New York,

were treated to ice cream. Most had never seen it before, and they spread the cold "new butter" on their bread with knives.

What if the world's population continues to double every 37 years, as it has been? In 900 years there would be 30 *million billion* people!

On every square yard of the earth's surface, both land and sea, 100 people would be standing on top of each other. Continuous buildings the size of the Empire State Building would not hold them all.

Beat this: Nothing in the Constitution prevents a public school teacher from paddling a pupil. That's what the Supreme Court ruled in April, 1977.

Why hasn't anyone seen Santa Claus?

One reason is that he is fast. Oh, so *fast!*

Two scholars at the University of Chicago worked out Santa's lightning in-and-out course.

With nearly 2 billion homes to visit around the world, his reindeer must speed him some 100 million miles during Christmas Eve.

By going in the same direction as the earth turns, he makes use of 24 hours of night. But even if he spends only a half of 1/10,000 second at each home, he has only half an hour left for traveling.

So he can't slow down. He must whiz through the sky at 70,000 miles per second, or 40 percent of the speed of light. Maybe that's why no one has ever seen him.

He hasn't even time for a single "Ho!"

Naturally, some "expert" said that "Ho, ho, ho" frightens little children. So many department store Santa Clauses have switched to, "Hello, there. I've been expecting you."

Did you know that you can buy candy in more places in the United States than you can buy a loaf of bread?

Two Voyager spacecraft have been launched to study our solar system. They will then head out across the galaxy. Along with scientific equipment, the Voyagers carry information about life on earth in 1977.

In about 100,000 years a Voyager may reach the nearest star. To beings there, it will show 20th-century humans at a time as far distant from us as we are from the cave-dwelling Neanderthal man.

The longest word in the Old Testament is in Isaiah 8:1,3—*Mahershalalhashbaz.*

If all the waters of the seas were spread evenly over the earth's surface, they would cover hills, valleys, and ocean floors to a depth of 9,000 feet. That is a layer of water 6 times as high as the Sears Tower in Chicago, the world's tallest building.

In the time it takes you to read 25 words, 4 people somewhere in the world will have starved to death— most of them children.

Change of pace. . . .
If you live in a big city, you probably walk about twice as fast as a person in a small town.
The average big-city dweller walks 5.5 feet per second, fast enough to travel 50 feet in 9.1 seconds. People in the smallest towns average 2.7 feet per second, or 50 feet in 18.4 seconds.

Since 1960 the great Sahara desert in North Africa has been moving south at the rate of 5.5 miles a year.
Don't be alarmed. When it gets to the sea, it's licked.

Three professors in Puerto Rico announced in 1977 that they had developed a cheat-proof examination sheet. The sheets are darkened with a light-reflecting ink of pale blue.

It is impossible, say the professors, for a student to copy the answer of another student seated next to him under normal classroom conditions.

Little Noahn facts. . . .

Scholars believe that Noah's Ark was a rectangular box larger than 20 basketball courts.

It was about 450 feet long, 75 feet wide, and 45 feet high—large enough to hold 568 railroad freight cars or nearly 30,000 animals.

The ark was meant merely to float. So it had no rudder, sails, or oars.

Shipbuilders discovered that the relationship of its

length to its width, 6 to 1, was so stable that the United States battleship *Oregon* was built to the same proportions.

A baby is born every 7 seconds.

Six sextillion five hundred eighty-eight quintillion tons. That's 6,588,000,000,000,000,000,000.

What in the world is so heavy? Easy—the earth.

And it's gaining weight every minute. Up to 10 tons of space dust fall on us daily.

Yet earth is a mere speck in space. More than 1 million earths could fit into the sun.

President Carter's budget called for the government to spend more than half a trillion dollars in 1979.

To be exact, $500,174,000,000.

With that amount of money you could have given about $7 to every person who has lived and died in the past 500,000 years.

There was approximately 1 car for every 2 people in the United States in 1975. In the same year there was only 1 car for every 5,711 people in China.

Ten thousand years ago there were more lions on earth than human beings.

And they probably had a roaring good time.

Tomato ketchup pours slowly because of "thixo-tropy."

That means it doesn't know whether it is a liquid or a solid. Honey, toothpaste, face cream, and mayonnaise are also thixotropic.

Now that you understand, never swear at a ketchup bottle. Just say "Thixotropic!"

In 1970, a year after Neil Armstrong landed on the moon, American motorists drove one trillion one hundred twenty-five billion (1,125,000,000,000) miles, just enough to make 4.5 million trips to the moon.

How do you make 24 states disappear?

Simple.

First you put Rhode Island, Connecticut, and Hawaii into New Hampshire.

Then you fit New Hampshire, New Jersey, Massachusetts, Vermont, Maryland, South Carolina, and West Virginia into Nevada.

Next you pack Nevada, Maine, Indiana, Kentucky, Delaware, and New York into Texas.

Finally you squeeze Texas, Ohio, Virginia, Tennessee, Pennsylvania, Mississippi, Louisiana, and Alabama into Alaska.

Now if you could only hide Alaska in Rhode Island.

Bicycles outsold automobiles in the United States from 1972 through 1976—58.7 million to 48.8 million—according to the Bicycle Manufacturers Association of America.

The yearly cost of keeping a criminal in prison is greater than that of keeping a student in college.

On the average a 4-year-old child asks 437 questions a day.

The United States government's Travel Service publishes a guide for ghost fans. It's called *The Supernatural—Haunted Houses and Legendary Ghosts*. Listed are 29 places where you might see what you really don't want to.

Sink your teeth into this one: In 1977 Americans chewed $1 billion worth of gum. The same amount of money would have paid the year's dental bills of all the boys and girls under 19 living east of the Mississippi River.

Popeye began as a free-swearing sailor in a comic strip meant for grown-ups.

In 1931 newspaper publisher William Randolph Hearst realized that the new strip was gaining unexpected favor with children. He asked Popeye to watch his language.

This will floor you. The average elevator travels 10,000 miles each year, roughly the distance between Washington, D.C., and Melbourne, Australia.

In *really* high buildings, such as the World Trade

Center in New York City, elevators travel as far as 35,000 miles a year.

Blue and white are the most common school colors.

A shocking amount of mail is sent to Americans asking them to buy something. One estimate is that 22 billion pieces of "junk" mail are sent yearly— enough to fill 55,000 nine-room, two-car-garage houses from floor to ceiling.

Swimming pools in Phoenix, Arizona, pick up 20 pounds of dust a year.

In case you hadn't noticed, the earth is slowing down.
Since 1972 the International Astronomical Union has added 1 second to the end of each year to keep our clocks straight.
If something hadn't been done, the official times around the world would be a whole day off in 37,000 years, more or less.
Now just wait a second. . . .

Coolest kid: On January 7, 1978, Emilio Palma became the first child ever born on the icy continent of Antarctica.

The winged pea, unknown until 1974, may be the answer to starvation. All its parts can be eaten—roots, flowers, and shoots. Even the stalks can be used to feed animals.

Carvings by Daniel Boone may still be seen on a 300-year-old beech tree near the Forked Deer River in Tennessee. The carvings include 2 crescent moons, 3 sets of initials, a bare foot, and "D. Boone, 1776."

The other initials on the tree—E. B., M. S., and M. C.—apparently belong to Edward Boone, Daniel's

brother, and two companions, Mike Stoner and Mike Calloway.

But Dan'l is still top-notch.

There is storage for 90 million pounds of cocoa beans in Hershey, Pennsylvania—enough to make 5.5 million chocolate bars.

Girls who don't look forward to housekeeping can be thankful they weren't born 100 years ago, when more than half the working women were maids or cooks.

The first message tapped by Samuel Morse over his invention the telegraph was, "What hath God wrought?"

The first words spoken by Alexander Bell over his invention the telephone were, "Watson, please come here. I want you."

The first words spoken by Thomas Edison into his invention the phonograph were, "Mary had a little lamb."

Seems nobody has the last word.

Americans who went to college usually take better care of their children than those who didn't.

Peas are the oldest known vegetable.

A girl born in 1974 can expect to live to be 76. A boy born in 1974 can expect to live to be 68.

The largest stamp ever printed in the United States is the Adolph Ochs 13-cent, issued in New York City on September 13, 1976. It is 1.05 inches by 1.80 inches. The smallest is the Indian Head Penny Experimental Reduced Size 13-cent stamp, issued on

January 11, 1978, in Kansas City, Missouri. It is .54 inches by .66 inches.

During 1971, in California alone, $22.3 million worth of bicycles were stolen.

Snips and snails and puppy tails, not sugar and spice.
Half the wives in the United States who want children favor boys. Only a third prefer girls.

Show me the way to go home. As of 1975 there were 3,800,000 miles of roads in the United States.

Shazam! A copy of *Marvel Comics* Number 1 sold for $7,500 at a convention of comic book collectors in New York City on July 8, 1977. No joke.
The previous comic book sale record: $5,000 paid in 1976 for an issue of *Action Comics* with one of the first Superman adventures.

Hold the water. Restaurants in the United States serve 70 million meals a day. Every glass of water brought to your table requires another 2 glasses to wash and rinse it.

So by not asking for water unless you are thirsty, you can help save about 7 million gallons daily.

The first American schoolbook, the *New England Primer*, was printed in Boston, Massachusetts, in 1689.

Enough ships exist to bear off to sea all the cars, buses, trucks, and motorcycles in the world.

Wood automobile tires were tested during World War II when rubber was in short supply. They rode smoothly enough at speeds up to 75 miles per hour over good roads, but chipped when they hit a hole.

Wooden you know.

The 3 words in the English language with the letters *uu* are: vacuum, residuum, and continuum.

Now that you know, say thank you.

You're welcuum.

The moon moves 2 inches farther from the earth each year.

Nine presidents did not go to college: Washington, Jefferson, Van Buren, Taylor, Fillmore, Lincoln, Johnson (Andrew), Cleveland, and Truman.

The 10 most common last names in the United States are, in order: Smith, Johnson, Williams, Brown, Jones, Miller, Davis, Wilson, Anderson, and Taylor.

The most *uncommon* name? Zzyzzx. Hero Zzyzzx lives in Madison, Wisconsin. His father, Xerxes Zzyzzx, named him after the man pictured on the pack of Players cigarettes, a man named Hero.

William is the most popular first name for males.

If you're unhappy with your first name, think how much worse it could be. For example, how'd you like Truewilllaughinglifebuckyboomermanifestdestiny? That's what a Florida baby was named. His middle name is George James.

Not bad, really. Think of the size of the birthday cake!

You can be sent to jail for 30 days or fined up to $100 for carrying a toy gun in Dubuque, Iowa.

Mark Twain bought one of the earliest typewriters. He became the first American author to deliver a typewritten book manuscript to a publisher—the book was *Life on the Mississippi*.

For skating fans. Ice covers roughly 10 percent of the earth's land surface—about the same amount as farms.

Numbers don't lie. . . ?
Colgate University found that students did better

at math when they were lying down than when they sat at desks.

With pillows under their feet (but not under their heads), a group of students figured math problems 7.4 percent more quickly and 14 percent more accurately.

In a normal lifetime an American will eat 200 pounds of peanuts and 10,000 pounds of meat, and drink 27,900 quarts of milk.

Is smaller safer? Big cars may be less dangerous in a smash-up, but small cars get into fewer accidents.

A tie-dy price: In 1977—when more than 7 million Americans didn't have jobs—a company in New York City sold 36 neckties at $3,000 apiece. Sewn into each necktie were diamonds and a gold rose.

Telephone engineers report: The normal speech rate is 350 words for the first 3 minutes of a long-distance telephone call if one person does all the yakking.

You can say a lot in 350 words and even be wise. Abraham Lincoln needed only 267 words for his famous Gettysburg Address.

Among junior and senior high school students, seventh graders are the most likely to commit acts of violence and vandalism.

When Lyndon Johnson was President, he created a booklet to be sent to the thousands of children who wrote to the White House asking for information about the First Family.

While the booklets about Presidents Johnson, Nixon, and Ford were prepared mainly for high school students, President Carter's booklet was aimed at elementary school kids. And it added questions and answers.

Among the most frequent questions asked by children:

"How many gates are there to the White House?" Answer: 11.

"How many pets live in the White House?" Answer: During the Carter years there was a dog named Grits and a cat named Misty Malarky Ying Yang.

"Children want to know things that would never occur to an adult," said Mrs. Nan Powell, coauthor of the Carter booklet.

Presidents receive between 3,000 and 4,000 letters a week from elementary school kids.

For playing the role of the monster in the original *Frankenstein* movie in 1931, Boris Karloff was paid only $125 a week.

Corniest fact: Americans bought 3 million electric corn poppers in 1974.

A new book is published in the United States every 13 minutes.

Lucy Hayes, wife of our nineteenth President, was the first First Lady to have a college education.

Sometimes facts are all wet. For instance, raindrops fall in many sizes. Some are 10 times larger than others.

Bloodlines of twelve United States Presidents, up to and including Richard Nixon, can be traced back to kings.

Antarctica is the only continent which has never been bloodied by the wars of man.

Happy birthday. The most recently discovered star is only 2,000 to 3,000 years old, less than a tenth the age of the next youngest known star.

Named Becklin–Neugebauer, after its discoverers, the new star is 20 million miles across the center, compared to earth's 7,926 miles, and it's 20 times heavier than the sun.

The average weight of a cubic foot of snow is 15 pounds.

Thinking about a career? You might find one you like in the *Dictionary of Occupational Titles*. The dictionary is put out by the Department of Labor. It lists 20,000 jobs.

There's a job for everyone. How about "pickle pumper" or "sunglass clip attacher"?

If you like clothing, look into "wearing apparel shaker." That's a person who shakes out clothing for ironing, sorting, or folding.

Even the Treasurer of the United States doesn't know exactly how much money is passing from person to person and place to place in the country on any day.

Best guess: $87,261,763,390 in paper bills and $9,768,188,598 in coins.

That's called passing the buck.

The world's most powerful telescope is in Russia. If it were put on the North Pole, it could spy a match flame burning on the South Pole.

Go west, young man. California, which brought you hula hoops and skateboards, has the greatest number of mopeds.

More women than men were enrolled in American colleges in 1977.

If all the people in the United States were as crowded together as the people on Manhattan Island are, they would still fit easily into the tiny state of Delaware.

Model builders buy 50 million plastic model kits a year. Model cars lead in popularity—35 percent of sales—followed by trucks and trailers, airplanes, spacecraft, ships, and military vehicles.

America's best-selling ice cream flavor isn't chocolate—it's vanilla. Oh, fudge!

Only about 30 states celebrate Lincoln's Birthday.

People in Hawaii live 4 years longer on the average than Americans in other states.

Comic books were first published in 1904. They were made up of colored cartoons that had appeared earlier in newspapers.

Ten inches high and 15 inches wide, each comic book was 40 pages long and sold for 75 cents. Among the first titles were *Lulu and Leander*, *Happy Hooligan*, and *The Katzenjammer Kids*.

In 1976 manufacturers sold $196 million worth of stuffed toys.

Frankly speaking, Americans eat about 18 billion hot dogs a year.

The number of children's books with black people as characters doubled in the 10 years ending in 1975. Even so, blacks appeared in only 1 out of every 7 children's books published.

One of the most remarkable dollhouses in the world was named in honor of a fairy queen. It took

15 years to build and furnish down to the smallest lamp and picture.

Sir Neville Wilkinson, an author of children's stories, got the idea from his 3-year-old daughter, Guendolen, in 1907. She told him that she had spied fairies dancing by the roots of a tree outside their home in Dublin, Ireland.

Sir Neville had the house modeled for the royal family of fairydom, whose queen was Titania.

Titania's Palace is 12 feet long, 8 feet wide, and 6 feet high and surrounds a courtyard. The 16 rooms, including a throne room, are lit and heated by electricity.

In 1967 Guendolen sold the dollhouse for $88,200. On January 10, 1978, it was resold for $256,500.

Eat your words.

A man from a candy company spends months with kids of elementary and junior high school ages.

What he hears winds up on next year's Valentine candy—messages such as "O.U. Duke," "Hang Ten," "No Way," and "Hit the Road."

Running commentary. A diesel engine locomotive is never shut off unless it needs repairs.

Diet news: Every day the sun loses 360 million tons of weight.

Americans eat an average of 134 pounds of sugar a year.

On January 31, 1977, there was snow on the ground in a part of every one of the 49 mainland states for the first time on record.

Get 'em up, Scout. Membership in the Boy Scouts of America dropped from an all-time high of 4.8 million in 1972 to 3.5 million in 1976.

Eamon P. Cronin, Jr., 10, of Wethersfield, Connecticut, can blow bubbles underwater through his eyes. The bubbles come out the corners near his nose. His star is Pisces, or the fish, but he says he's no boy from Atlantis.

When Keith Hefner of Ann Arbor, Michigan, was 15, he formed Youth Liberation, Inc. The group championed kids' lib.

Among other things, it supported giving children the vote and the right to divorce their parents and get alimony.

Somehow it failed to catch on.

When last heard from, Keith was fighting the battle alone.

"I'm not giving up on this yet," he said.

Teen power: Tony Asaro, 16, and Jeff Cole, 14, both of Santa Rosa, California, got tired of waiting while city officials bickered over plans for a $7,000 footbridge. So early in 1977 the boys built the bridge themselves—for free.

Kim Hunter of Lansing, Michigan, taught himself to read at the age of 3 and was a high school student at age 7. In 1977, at the age of 11, he enrolled at Michigan State University, having scored in the top 5 percent on the freshman entrance exams.

No loss for words. Michael Miller became a "college professor" at the age of 15. In 1977 the tenth grader began teaching at New York City's New School for Social Research. His course, "Beyond Crossword Puzzles," dealt with difficult types of puzzles. Michael's teaching fee: $550.

Home delivery: When Keiichi Stevens was born on January 10, 1977, the "doctor" was his brother Jimmy, 13. Jimmy delivered Keiichi in their home in Anaheim, California, while another brother, Chuckie, 8, relayed instructions telephoned in by a police sergeant.

"He told me to pull the baby out gently, clear his mouth, and make sure he was breathing," said Jimmy.

Animal crackers ride herd on education. Until they're 10, many kids believe a bear is as tall as a giraffe.

Americans would escape 630,000 injuries and 11,500 deaths yearly if 7 out of 10 car riders wore seat belts. Only about 2 out of 10 put them on.

An army of 3,000 model lead soldiers was sold in 1977 for $16,000. The soldiers belonged to Douglas Fairbanks, Jr., age 67, an actor. He began his collection at the age of 12.

One group was a military band of 21 Royal Marines in red jackets, white trousers, and pith helmets. Made in 1938, the group cost $1.50 new. It sold for $1,392.00.

I CAN'T BLAME THIS YOUNG TEENAGER. I HOLD YOU, THE PARENTS, RESPONSIBLE FOR MY TORN ROBE.

Parents in Chicago can be held responsible for unlawful acts by their children. The parents can be made to pay not only the cost of the damaged property, but also the court fines, which range up to $500.

The Nutley Chapter of the Millard Fillmore Society cares about the underdog. Each year it awards a scholarship to some high school student who has less than a C average.

Don't pan pizza. Children at Florida elementary schools were asked in 1977 to vote for their favorite food from among four choices: pizza, tacos, hamburgers, and hot dogs. Pizza won handily.

Public schools across the nation served an average of 941,619 lunches daily in October, 1977, up from 929,732 in October, 1976.

Collectors of postage stamps in the United States number more than 16 million.

Howard Hughes was one of the wealthiest men in the world when he died on April 5, 1976. His holdings were worth $1 billion. But he left only $1,799 in cash.

In the mid-1940s a New York City daily newspaper printed 20 inches of radio listings and 2 inches of television listings every day.

It may not be an earthshaking question, but have you ever wondered where paper clips go?

Lloyd's Bank of London kept track of 100,000 paper clips. Only about 20,000 were used to clip papers together.

Of the others, 14,163 were twisted during conversations on the telephone, 19,143 were used as card game chips, 7,200 held clothing together, 5,423 were used to pick teeth or scratch ears, 5,308 cleaned fingernails, 3,916 unplugged tobacco pipes. The remaining 25,000 were swept into the trash after falling onto the floor.

Twenty years after the Russians sent the first Sputnik into space in 1957, some 6,070 man-made objects had fallen out of orbit. About 4,595 were still floating.

The sky is not yet cluttered. The distance between one moving object and another is still great. Put into earth terms, it's like looking down a highway and spying a bubble-gum wrapper 50 miles away.

Gym Dandies

One for all. In a junior high school basketball game in Illinois in 1962, both teams had the *same* high scorer.

Ted Kern not only led his Terre Haute team to a 13–2 victory. He also sank a shot into the wrong basket.

Two 11-year-old girls hold the record for the longest point in a regular tennis match.
Cari Hagey and Colette Kavanagh, both of La Jolla, California, hit the ball across the net 1,029 times.
The point was played in the seventh game of the second set of the finals of the Anaheim Junior Tennis Tournament on November 11, 1977, and took 51.5 minutes.
Cari won, 2–6, 6–4, 6–2, in five hours.

The wheel facts: Skateboard injuries have soared to 350,000 a year. About 100,000 victims need hospital treatment. Between 1975 and 1977 alone there were 28 deaths.

John Hodges, 16, of Trenton, New Jersey, a 147-pound amateur boxer, won his first Golden Gloves fight in record time.
In a bout on January 20, 1964, he knocked out his opponent in the first second of the first round.
Time of the bout, including the referee's 10-count: 11 seconds.

The only woman to break a world's athletic record held by a man was swimmer Sybil Bauer, 19.

On October 7, 1922, in Hamilton, Bermuda, she backstroked 440 yards in 6:24.8, beating the men's record of 6:28.0 held by Harold Krueger of Honolulu. During the race she also broke the records at 300 and 400 yards.

Possibly the best female swimmer of all time, she once held all the existing women's backstroke records. Her career was cut short by cancer, and she died on January 31, 1927, at the age of 23.

Although he finished 48 minutes behind the winner in the New York City Marathon on October 23, 1977, Wesley Paul got his share of the headlines.

Wesley, only 8, ran the 26 miles 385 yards in 3

hours 31 seconds, lowering his own world age-group record by 15 minutes. It was his fifth marathon.

Hail the conkering heroes!

To most Japanese, golf was fairly new in 1958—and as safe as standing under a rockslide.

There were 1,200,000 golfers and 37,400 girl caddies in the country. The golfers hadn't learned to straighten out their shots, and the girl caddies hadn't learned to duck.

More than 500 girls were conked cold during the year before they took to wearing helmets.

Nobody's perfect. Nonetheless, the All Saints High School reserves were close to it when they beat St. Casimir's reserves in a basketball game in Detroit in 1957. The score: 62–0.

Said Father Paul Sierocki, athletic director at St. Casimir's: "I wanted to call it a day after the third quarter . . . but we're building for next year."

On October 4, 1977, John York, 16, swam the 21 miles from the California shore to Catalina Island in 8.5 hours, trying to be the first man to make the round trip. He collapsed 200 yards from his goal and was hauled from the water.

Still, he was happy, thinking he'd broken the record. He had, though only the men's. He came within 1.5 hours of matching the women's record, set the month before by Penny Dean. She made it both ways.

But the girls don't rule the water—yet.

In July, 1977, an English boy, David Morgan, 13, swam the English Channel, cutting more than 1 hour and 3 weeks off the old record.

David swam from Dover, England, to Wissant, France, in 11 hours 5 minutes. He was 3 weeks younger than Abla Khairi, an Egyptian girl who was also 13 when she made the crossing in 1974 in 12 hours 30 minutes.

Softball began as indoor baseball. The first game was played in a boat club in Chicago on November 30, 1887. The ball was a boxing glove, and batters used a broomstick for a bat.

Franklin Jacobs, 20, a sophomore at Fairleigh Dickinson University in Rutherford, New Jersey, jumped a record 23¼ inches above his head to set a world indoor high-jump mark on January 27, 1978.

Only 5 feet 8 inches, Franklin cleared 7 feet 7¼ inches on his third try at the Millrose Games in Madison Square Garden, New York City.

That equals a jump of 8 feet 3 inches for a man 6 feet 2 inches tall.

More than 3 million soccer balls were sold in 1977, as against only 500,000 in 1973.

Shy, slender (105 pounds) Karen Yvette Muir, 12, of Kimberly, South Africa, traveled to a swim meet in Blackpool, England, in 1965 just to gain experience. She had no real idea of how to start or turn.

Yet in the meet on August 10 she swam the 110-yard backstroke in 1:08.7. The time broke the world's record by .07 second. Karen thereby became the youngest person to hold a world's record in any event in a major sport.

Her happy mother telephoned from South Africa. She told Karen that she could spend her entire allowance in a celebration.

Dunk shot.

If you piled all the players in the National Basketball Association in 1977 one on top of the other, they would stand 23,060 inches tall. The topmost man could look down upon 12 Statues of Liberty standing on each other's shoulders.

What's in a name? Sometimes . . . well, not enough.

In 1963 the basketball coach of the Boys' Training School in Kearney, Nebraska, figured he had a high

scorer in a tall Indian youth. The youth's name: John Never Miss a Shot.

John, however, decided he liked baseball better.

Robert Lockhart was arrested for hitting a golf ball around a sheep's pasture in Central Park, New York City. As a result, in 1888 he helped found the first golf course in the United States, the 6-hole St. Andrews Golf Club in Yonkers, New York.

Buddy Gore, 16, of Wilmington, North Carolina, pitched a no-hitter in a 1961 Pony League game— and lost, 8–3.

Buddy walked 9 batters and let opposing players steal 10 bases. His catcher was charged with 9 passed balls.

The basketball game was the 1963–1964 season's opener for both Oregon high schools.

The first half was nip and tuck, with Redmond ahead of Madras, 22–20.

In the second half the Redmond boys thought they were living through a nightmare. They shot from the key; they drove for lay-ups; they lofted long ones. They missed and missed and missed. Fourteen free throws were tried and missed.

The final score was Madras 48, Redmond 22.

But wait!

Redmond's Kerry Parkinson had been fouled at the buzzer. The game over, he relaxed and calmly sank the throw for his team's only point in the second half.

Wait again. The basket didn't count. He had stepped over the foul line.

Third basemen in the major leagues live longer than their teammates.

Nancy Isenhour, 19, was the country's first girl to play on a men's college varsity basketball team. In

1945 Nancy played guard for High Point College in High Point, North Carolina. Although a substitute, she was considered the team's best set-shot.

Two hundred ninety-four thousand high school girls participated in sports of all kinds in 1971. By 1977 the figure had climbed to 1.6 million.

Matt Rogers of St. Albans, West Virginia, became the world's youngest holder of a karate black belt on June 26, 1976—12 days before his seventh birthday. He had studied karate since he was 4.

A Peewee League baseball game in Artesia, New Mexico, was called after 2 innings.

Officials were as tired as the 7-year-old players. Final score of the game, played in 1962, was Pirates 43, Dodgers 22.

Welch (West Virginia) High School's 1977 Homemaker of the Year Award went to William "Butch" Lindsay, an all-state football player at running back. He scored the highest in the school in a written test. Pass the pigskin, please.

Distance runner Julie Shea of Raleigh, North Carolina, set national mile records for her age group at 10, 11, 12, 13, 16, and 17. Her time as a 12-year-old was 5:01.4.

In 1977, at the age of 18, she broke her own high school record for the mile with a 4:43.1 clocking, and the women's 10-mile record with a time of 56:08.

Six-million-dollar boy.

Tall in the saddle is Steve Cauthen, though he stands only 5 feet 1 inch.

Steve became a jockey in November, 1976, when he was 16. The following year he rode a record 488 winning horses, whose purses totaled $6 million, also a record. He was named 1977's Athlete of the Year by the Associated Press and by *Sports Illustrated*.

Probably the greatest schoolboy football player of all time was Kenneth Hall of Sugar Land, Texas. He was 6 feet 1 inch, weighed 205 pounds, and ran the 100-yard dash in 9.7 seconds.

From 1950 to 1953 Kenneth rushed for 11,232 yards and scored 899 points. In one game he had 678 total yards, 7 touchdowns, and 13 extra points.

Diamonds are forever, but soccer fields are close.

The longest 1-day school soccer game was played on September 17, 1977, in the Adirondacks, New York. With 1:06 remaining in the fourteenth overtime period, Brian Wells of tiny Indian Lake High School scored to defeat even tinier Hague High, 3–2.

Once more with feeling.

The most evenly matched soccer teams in history were from St. Brigid's and Sacred Heart, 2 elementary schools in Baltimore, Maryland.

In 1958 the teams met 4 times. The first 3 games ended 1–0, 0–1, and 0–0. The fourth and deciding game took 3 days.

After 4 ten-minute overtimes, 2 five-minute overtimes, and a fifteen-minute "sudden death" period, the teams were tied, 1–1. Because of darkness officials decided to replay the game the next day.

The second day was almost a repeat—2 five-minute overtimes and a sudden death period. Still no winner.

On the third day Pat Brooks of St. Brigid's scored the winning goal a few minutes before the end of the regulation game.

"At least the boys have made lasting friendships," said a weary bystander.

Check your baseball cards for a picture of old-time shortstop Honus Wagner. You might strike it rich. In 1977 two men found a 1909 card of Wagner in a dusty antique shop. They bought it for 40 cents. It's worth $3,000.

Frederick Garcia III of Los Alamitos, California, is a real-life water baby. In June, 1977, he became the youngest person to pass the Red Cross water safety beginner's test. He was 8 months old.

Taft High in Cincinnati, Ohio, is the only school to have an entire backfield go on to play pro football. In the early 1960s Al Nelson, Cid Edwards, and Walter Johnson were starters, and Carl Ward was a sub.

It isn't how you play the game, it's. . . .
Borstal is where the law in England sends bad boys.

Now and then the people who run the place allow a few trusted boys out to play a game of rugby.

So it happened in January, 1978. The Borstal boys met a local team in Durham and were beaten, 68–0.

Never mind defeat, be it ever so crushing.

After the game the 15 Borstal boys ran off the field —and kept running.

"Perhaps they were downhearted after such a heavy loss and couldn't face going back," said a Borstal officer. "Normally our players are such good sports."

High school freshman Chris Phillips of Albany, New York, was banned from playing on the football team in 1977. It was ruled that his artificial leg might hurt someone.

Chris took his case to the New York State Public School Athletic Association. The ruling was overturned, and Chris was allowed to play.

Tracy Austin of Palos Verdes, California, never lost a tennis match to a girl her own age since she was 7.

By 1978 Tracy, 14, had won 153 tournaments. She became the youngest girl to be invited to Wimbledon, where she reached the third round; the youngest to reach the quarterfinals at Forest Hills; and the youngest to win the national 18-and-under championship.

Regina Barnes, 14, of Modesto, California, became the youngest life master in bridge, a card game. She was awarded her title in 1976 by the American Contract Bridge League.

While playing, Regina chewed gum and blew bubbles to help her to concentrate.

Stick with it, Regina!

A football game lasts 60 minutes.

However, the amount of time actually spent with the players in motion is far less.

Rarely is the total "motion time"—the time between the snap of the ball and the whistle that blows the play dead—more than 15 minutes.

In bowl games at the end of the 1977 season, motion time in the Orange Bowl was unofficially clocked at 13:44; in the Cotton Bowl, 14:19; and in the Gator Bowl, 14:27.

Tall story: A printer's error in a 1976 basketball program brought invitations from colleges all over the country to Bobby Kilgore of Central High School in Omaha, Nebraska.

Bobby was listed as 6 feet 11¼ inches, fourth tallest senior in the country. Being only 6 feet 1½ inches, or 10 inches short of his published height, he turned down the invitations.

"I didn't want to shock them," he said.

Ups and downs. The New York Giants football team defeated Green Bay 10–7 in 1933 and Washington 14–7 in 1942 without making a first down in either game.

Before a basketball game against the Chicago Bulls, John Havlicek of the Boston Celtics strapped on a pedometer, a device that measures the distance the wearer walks or runs.

Havlicek discovered that in the 43 minutes he played, he had traveled 8 miles.

David Renk of Alamo, Texas, was forbidden to play football because it was too dangerous.

So he took up bullfighting.

In January, 1978, David, 14, made his debut in Reynosa, Mexico. He succeeded with several smooth cape passes, but failed in three attempts at a kill.

Even so, he became the youngest American to go for the kill of a bull in Mexico.

Golf's craziest round was played in California over a "golf course" of 42 miles, running from Pasadena to Palmdale.

The golf-a-thon began as an argument between

Jim Rogers and Leonard Nash over who was the better golfer.

"I can beat you playing over a mountain," said Nash.

The nearest mountain is a crest that separates Greater Los Angeles from the desert.

On October 28, 1954, the men teed off from a street corner. Each man carried only 2 clubs—a 4-iron and a putter.

As night fell on the third day of play, Rogers, who had lost 128 balls, wiped his hands and took careful aim. Then he chipped into the "hole," a mop pail set in the doorway of a Palmdale café.

He had won by 2 strokes, 678 to 680.

But loser Nash had the longest drive—5,000 feet into a mile-deep canyon.

A British Army officer, Major Walter Clopton Wingfield, is regarded as the inventor of tennis. In 1873 he introduced "tennis-on-the-lawn" at a garden party in Wales.

The net was 5 feet high, and the court was shaped like an hourglass.

Where the action isn't . . . .

Florence snuffed Crandon 2–1 in a regulation Wisconsin high school basketball game on January 21, 1977.

Yes, basketball.

Crandon jumped ahead 1–0 on a free throw by Ben Samz in the first quarter.

Immediately taking the ball out of bounds, Florence raced downcourt. Nick Baumgart threw in what proved to be the winning basket.

Thereafter Crandon went into a "delayed offense." The rest of the game was scoreless.

After grabbing the fourth quarter tip, Crandon held on to the ball. With 4 seconds left they attempted the go-ahead basket, and missed.

The 32-minute game boasted only 7 field goal attempts. Winner Florence had the ball on offense a mere 32 seconds, or 1/60 of the time.

"A game like this sure shoots heck out of our offensive average," said Florence coach Stan Jesky. "But I guess it helps our defensive average."

The year before, Crandon had won, 95–78.

It's against the law to play marbles for keeps in Ashland, Wisconsin.

Brent Bogle of Santa Ana, California, is the youngest long-distance runner. He ran 30 miles in 6 hours 3 minutes at the age of 4.

Dee Dee Neil was the heroine of the game as Leroy defeated Quenemo 83–1 in a girls' high school basketball game in Kansas on January 4, 1977. Even the referee shook Dee Dee's hand.

Dee Dee was high scorer—for Quenemo.

In the time it takes a man to swim 137 yards, a shark can swim a mile.

Rebecca Ann Chase, 8, of Dallas, Oregon, scored a hole-in-one on the first hole she ever played.

Using a shortened 3-wood, she sank her tee shot on the 125-yard par-3 fifth hole of the Oak Knoll Golf course on August 15, 1977.

"She wasn't half as excited as her father," said the golf course's owner, Mike Payette. "She thought that was what you're supposed to do, put the ball in the hole."

The shot made her the youngest girl ever to score an ace.

Hats off—or rather, hat off—to baseball pitcher Dennis Gibbs of Fortuna High School, Fortuna, California.

In a game at Del Norte High on April 26, 1977, as Dennis pitched the ball, a gust of wind blew off his cap. The ball landed in the cap on the way to the plate.

Cap and ball traveled together a yard or so before the wind floated the cap to the shortstop.

The ball dropped 20 feet in front of the plate and slightly to the left. Then it rolled slowly through a gate and out of the ball park.

All runners advanced 1 base. Fortuna lost, 15–5.

You won't find a husky lady named Hessie Dona-hue in the books on the manly art of boxing. But

Hessie knocked out the then heavyweight champ of the world, John L. Sullivan, in a ring in Arkansas.

The track and field record that lasted longest was for the 50-mile walk. It was set in 1878 by G. B. Gille. His time of 9:29:22 was not broken until 1966, eighty-eight years later, when Shaul Ladany of Israel walked the distance in 8:35:35.

Back in 1967 Charlene Rowe, 11, of Charlotte, North Carolina, made news because she pitched for an unbeaten, otherwise all-boy baseball team.

Ten years later girls all over the country thought nothing of playing against boys in every sport.

Today, half the kids in America say that whatever a boy can do, a girl can do better. Many girls did just that in 1977. Here are 6 standouts:

—Kristine Flores, 11, of East Hills, California, who led the Big Red of the East Hills Little League to its third straight championship. Kristine, a pitcher, had a 14–0 record, struck out 130 batters in 70 innings, threw a no-hitter, batted .509, and scored 52 RBIs.

—Leigha Gomaz, 11, of Wales, Wisconsin, who finished second in the fifth grade flyweight class at the Kettle Moraine Middle School wrestling tournament.

—Tana Hill, 11, of Poelika, Alabama, who made her basketball league's all-star team.

—Tracey Kennedy, 12, of Houston, Texas, who won her city's soccer skills contest for boys and girls 12 and under.

—Kelly Vickers, 12, of Monroe, Louisiana, who was a 2-way starter (linebacker and halfback) on the Logtown seventh grade football team.

—Karen Whritenour, 12, of Minneapolis, Minnesota, who ran the 220-yard dash faster than any boy in her school.

—Amber Edwina Hunt, 11, of Murray, Utah, who defeated all the boys she boxed, the first 8 by technical knockouts. Her secret weapon: weight lifting.

Super Bowl XII was watched by more people than any previous television program.

According to the Nielsen ratings, 104 million viewers saw Dallas defeat Denver in the 3-hour show on January 15, 1978.

In a high school basketball game against Shoreland Lutheran in Kenosha, Wisconsin, Laura Merisalo of University Lake played the last minute as a 1-girl team—and won.

Even before the game on January 12, 1978, Lake began losing players. Four of the 9 girls on the squad became sick with the flu.

Nevertheless Lake led at halftime, 22–11.

Then, in the second half, Lake players dropped out one after another.

First to go was Mary Allen, who departed with 5 fouls. Still Lake held a 25–16 third quarter lead.

Early in the fourth quarter Rita Landis was sidelined by a sprained ankle. Sandy Saeger fouled out. Ann Yoemans followed with a minute to play.

Laura Merisalo, with 4 fouls, was left to go it alone. Another foul meant Lake would have no players on the floor. It would have to forfeit the game.

In that last minute Laura was careful as well as fast. She held the Shoreland quintet to only 4 points, and Lake squeaked to a 33–29 victory.

One Lioners
and Bushy Tales

Pilot whales have been trained by the Navy to recover torpedoes and other objects as far beneath the surface of the sea as 1,600 feet.

One Pacific Coast oyster produces about 10 billion young a year. If all of them lived, in 5 generations they would make a ball 8 times as big as the world.

There are 1 million different kinds of bugs. They range from mites you can't see clearly without a magnifying glass to 9-foot spider crabs.

Bugs make up 78 percent of all creatures and weigh 12 times more than the whole human race.

Keeping up with the Joneses. Puppies eat 14 to 50 percent more food when fed in groups than when they are fed separately.

The two parts of animals that give off the most heat are the tail and the ears.

Some animals that live in warm areas have larger ears and tails than their cousins in colder areas. For example, a desert fox has long ears, while an Arctic fox has small ones.

You can tell a skunk is about if you smell only .000,000,000,000,071 ounce of its spray.

The rare calvaria tree is being saved by the turkey.

At one time there were only 13 such trees left on the island of Mauritius in the Indian Ocean. They were over 300 years old.

Their thick-shelled seeds had to be worn down by the dodo's digestive system before sprouting. But the dodo, a flightless bird, died out before the start of the eighteenth century.

Then along came Dr. Stanley A. Temple of the University of Wisconsin. He force-fed fresh calvaria seeds to turkeys, whose gizzards, like the dodos', have stones for crushing food.

Several days later 3 seeds sprouted.

"These may well be the first calvaria seeds to sprout in more than three hundred years," said Dr. Temple.

If a cockroach touches a human being, it runs off to safety and cleanses itself.

A cat or dog at 1 year is equal in age to a 15-year-old person. Roughly, cats or dogs at ages 3, 6, 9, 12, and 16 are 30, 40, 50, 65, and 80 years old respectively in terms of human age.

You may still see signs in Malaya asking you not to dance on the backs of giant turtles.

In 1962 the government had to put up the signs. Twinkle-toed tourists were scaring the turtles away from their last breeding grounds.

Lobsters weighing 10 pounds and more were once common off the shores of the United States. Those caught today seldom weigh even 2.5 pounds.

Should you meet a swarm of bees, don't scream. If bees smell your breath, they'll go down your open mouth and choke you.

Well, I'll bee.

Sharks can see 10 times better than human beings.

Animal breeders in Russia claim to have bred sheep with blue wool.

Why do dogs bury bones? Even scientists don't know. They doubt it is for storing food.

Creepy crawlers. The poisonous tarantula spider isn't for everybody. But consider its good points:

It can live 2 years without food and 7 months without water. And at your birthday party, you can say, "Come see my pet."

However, the cheapest pet is probably the snail. It can go 4 or 5 years without food.

Maybe that's why it moves so slowly.

Because of the value of their ivory tusks, elephants are being slaughtered. Of the 33 African countries in which they live, they are protected only by Somalia, Botswana, Rwanda, and South Africa.

The huge beasts are slain by rifles, by tribesmen setting fire to the long grass around the herds, and by rockets shot from helicopters.

In 1977 there were 1.3 million elephants left. That is not a lot. In 1976 alone, ivory from 100,000 to 400,000 elephants was shipped from Africa.

The biggest ivory market is Hong Kong, which in 1976 brought in 710 tons of ivory—the tusks of 71,000 elephants. A pair of tusks sells in Hong Kong for up to $2,800.

Keeping a pet the first year—even if it doesn't get sick—can cost your dad more than a headache. Food and equipment nibble away at the purse strings.

Here's what it cost in 1977 to keep a pet for the first year: parakeet, $62; gerbil or hamster, $80; fish, $140; kitten, $175 to $200; small puppy, $375; large puppy, $715; horse, $2,900.

Leopards and tigers may be endangered species in Asia, but not in America. They breed so easily in captivity that zoos don't want any more.

The *Johnsonia eriomma,* or "bigeye fish," has eyes that are one fifth as long as its body.

A man's eye in the same proportion would be more than a foot long and would stick out 8 inches.

The blue whale is the largest creature on earth.

It is bigger than 30 elephants and weighs more than 2,000 people. Its heart alone weighs 1,200 pounds.

Some of its blood vessels are so large that a small child could crawl through them.

What do you say to a bulldog in East Africa?
"Bow wow"?
Wrong.
Just as there are different languages, there are different sounds to describe the noises animals make.

A dog in East Africa says "woo woo," while a Japanese dog says "wan wan." In Bangkok a dog barks "bahk bahk." In Russia, "gahf gahft."

A cow in Thailand says "oo-ah." A cow in Arabia says "mah." In Japanese and Swahili, cows say "moh."

On the other hand most cats around the world say

"meeow." But a Japanese cat says "neow." Cats in Thailand and Lebanon agree on "mao."

"Oink" comes out of most pigs. However, Japanese pigs say "boo boo." Thailand pigs say "oot oot." Russian pigs utter "ha-roo."

Roosters would have the most trouble "talking" to their foreign cousins. Few say "cock-a-doodle-doo." Among the many ways they chase other roosters are "koo-koo-ruh-koo" in Germany, "ay-ee-ache-ache" in Thailand, "koh-koh-ee-oo-koh" in Kenya, and koo-koo-ruh-koo" in Ecuador.

Better stay at home.

Automobile drivers kill more game animals than hunters do.

The bolas spider spins its own rope and throws it around its prey.

The tick, a wingless insect, smells with its front legs.

In Tulsa, Oklahoma, land of oil wells, dogs run like greased lightning.

Molly Wolf was handed a $20 traffic ticket because her puppy was speeding. Blackie, her 4-month-old hound, exceeded the speed limit in November, 1977.

Blackie did 30 miles per hour in a 25-mile-per-hour zone running from the dogcatcher. He escaped into the Wolf house through a hole in the screen.

The city attorney tossed the case into the doghouse.

John Magrich, 4, defeated several dozen grown-ups to win the 1965 Los Angeles County Hog Calling contest.

The grown-ups strained with calls like "Pig, pig, pig, WHOOOoooeee, WHOOOoooeee, WHOOOoooeee, pig, pig, pig"; or "OOOOoooeeee, OOOOoooeeee, ERGH, ERGH, RRrkie, RRRoooeee, pig, pig, pig, piggy, RRROOOoooeee, ERGH, ERGH, RRROOOoooeeee."

John cried, "Here, piggy piggy," and 6 pigs walked right up to him.

Pound for pound the bonefish, which seldom grows larger than 9 pounds, is probably the strongest fish in the seas.

India has 50 million monkeys.

To a mouse, a house is a house. Even if it's the White House.

One afternoon President Carter saw a mouse race across his office rug. The General Services Administration, in charge of housekeeping, got the critter fast.

Soon afterward a second mouse popped up.

Has to be an "outside" mouse, declared the GSA.

"Outside" matters, including the White House grounds, are taken care of by the Department of the Interior. But they said the mouse wasn't theirs.

In the meantime the mouse died behind the walls.

An angry President called in the "outside" and

"inside" men and had them sniff. He told them to stop the excuses and get the darn thing out.

They did.

Penguins are the only birds that can leap in and out of the water like porpoises.

Count space pioneers among our forgotten heroes —particularly Ham.

On January 31, 1961, Ham whooshed 155 miles into the sky aboard a Redstone rocket. A short time later he splashed into the Atlantic and onto the front pages of the world.

Today Ham is a has-been.

He lives in the National Zoo in Washington, D.C.,

where he ranks only fifth in popularity. Visitors are more interested in the collection of ordinary monkeys, the Chinese pandas, Smokey the Bear, and 5 white tigers.

Ham, a 150-pound chimp, turned 20 in July, 1977. He'll probably live 15 or 20 more years. So there is still time to pay your respects to the aging hero.

Chinese medicine stores in Singapore sell animal parts for use as medicine. Most valuable is the powder made from the horn of a Java rhinoceros. An ounce sells for more than three times the price of gold.

By some unknown means the iguana, a type of lizard, can end its own life.

Americans spend about $3 billion for cat and dog food each year.

The elephant's trunk grows about 1 inch every million years.

Today the super nose is a tool second only to the hand of man.

It has 40,000 muscles. It's a spoon for feeding, a spade for digging, a hose for bathing, a direction finder for locating food or scenting danger. It can uproot a tree, pick up a pin, or untie a slipknot.

Spiders live on liquids. They must digest their food before eating it, so they shoot a powerful juice onto their prey.

Get a whiff of this. Giant skunks the size of German shepherd dogs were discovered in the jungles of Java in May, 1977. The big stinkers are believed to be survivors from prehistoric times.

A female deer with antlers, which were thought to grow on males only, was captured near Jackson, Wyoming, in January, 1978.

The FBI was not called in.

The saluki, which is closely related to the greyhound, is the oldest known breed of pet dog.

For heaven's snakes! The only states where poisonous snakes do not live are Alaska, Hawaii, and Maine. Snakes in the other 47 states bite some 45,000 people a year. However, only about 8,000 of these bites are poisonous.

Carriage horses in New Orleans must wear diapers.

To farmers long ago, it was a sign of snow if a cat sneezed, if game birds perched high in the trees, or if a dog had more fleas than usual.

Late update: Goats grazing on Mt. Nebo in Oregon are used by local people and radio station KRBS to foretell the weather.

The higher the goats climb up the 1,200-foot mountain, the better the weather will be.

Dogs bite a million Americans every year, but rarely to death. Of the 11 deaths in 1974 and 1975, nine of the victims were children under the age of 7.

Most likely to bite you is the German shepherd, followed by the chow chow, poodle, Italian bulldog, fox terrier, mixed chow chow, Airedale, Pekingese, and mixed German shepherd.

Dog bites peak in number during the middle of June. Then comes a sharp drop and a steady downturn as the cold weather moves in.

And stay out of Colorado Springs, Colorado, if you can't bite back. An old law gives a dog the right to one bite.

The greatest load ever pulled by a dog was a mining cart filled with concrete cylinders, a total weight of 7,000 pounds.

A 71-pound, 4-year-old yellow Labrador retriever named Bozo moved the cart 15 feet within the 90-second limit at the 1976 Alaska State Fair in Palmer.

Because of the ability to stretch their stomachs, angler fish can swallow prey twice their own size. Can you imagine a 50-pound kid gulping down a 100-pound candy bar?

The cowbird is so lazy it won't build a nest of its own. It lays and leaves its eggs in the nests of other birds.

Mosquitoes don't bother you in cool weather. The reason: they can't beat their wings when the temperature drops below 60 degrees.

All in the family. Scientists used to think that a shark gave birth to about 20 young at a time.

Then in 1967 seamen aboard the Soviet scientific ship *Vityaz* caught a tiger shark in the Indian Ocean. Scarcely had they hauled it onto the deck when it gave birth to 53 babies.

The poison of a black widow spider is 15 times more deadly than that of a rattlesnake.

Scientists are working on a way to clip the wings of ladybugs. Then the bugs will stay in one place and kill all the crop pests there.

Today there are between 15,000 and 17,000 different kinds of fish, 7,600 kinds of birds, and 4,500 kinds of mammals on earth.

Baboons have bum pitching arms. They can't throw overhand. Nevertheless, never trust a baboon carrying a rock. He probably means to drop it on you.

As a symbol of peace the dove has not led an easy life. Perhaps that's why a group of doves is called a pitying of doves.

Until 1977 about 100,000 porpoises were accidentally killed by tuna fishermen each year.

The air-breathing animals get caught in the nets along with the tuna and drown.

The Marine Mammal Protection Act of 1977 allowed a maximum of 62,429 deaths. In that year the tuna fishermen became more careful, and only 24,143 porpoises were killed.

The archer fish knocks flies off sea plants by shooting them with a drop of water.

No wonder the grasshopper can jump so high. It has about 100 more muscles than a human being.

The "pit viper" rattlesnake can tell a temperature change of as slight as 0.0001 degree.

Humans may someday have to communicate with beings from outer space. To learn how to go about

"talking" with strange creatures, scientists are practicing on animals.

At first the dolphin (porpoise) seemed the best bet. Its brain is very much like man's, though about 15 percent larger. But apes proved the easiest to teach.

The scientists use sign language, colors, and computer symbols. One chimp carried on a single hour of "talk" using 251 signs for words.

Chimps can even invent new expressions when needed. Examples are "finger bracelet" for ring, "water bird" for duck, and "juice fruit" for watermelon.

Koko, a gorilla, has a vocabulary of 300 to 450

words. A prize student, Koko's IQ is between 80 and 90.

Ducks may be at the bottom of the class.

Scientists at Drake University in Iowa ran up against a duck named Sir Lancelot. He knows only "peck" and "turn." And it appears the most he'll ever master is 5 to 7 words.

One problem is the long summer break. Over vacation, Sir Lancelot forgets his studies. He spends his time with his girlfriend, Lady Guinevere, a nonreader.

A kangaroo mother may weigh 60,000 times as much as its newborn baby. No wonder the babies are so jumpy.

The elephants at the Duzhanbe Zoo in Russia have had it. They are taking matters into their own trunks.

Vandals throw stones at them, and they throw them back. The zoo put up a warning sign: CAREFUL. THE ELEPHANTS THROW STONES. It didn't help.

For the next power failure. You can read a book beside an aquarium lighted by a single 3-inch *Photoblepharon palpebratus*, or flashlight fish.

Is your dog lonely? Does the poor pooch have trouble finding a date?

Mary Torrisi, 17, of Tampa, Florida, decided to help her pet.

She had the Great Dane's ear pierced and fitted with a trinket. Enter love. Dobbie, the boy dalmatian next door, went crazy over her.

Mary herself wears 3 earrings in her right ear and 2 in her left. She hopes someday to share a pair of diamond earrings with her dog.

When the worm turns. The American silkworm spins its cocoon out of a single thread almost a mile long.

Wasps were making paper millions of years before humans appeared on earth.

A mother octopus dies of starvation about 10 days after her eggs hatch.

"I know I hit it!" is the complaint of hunters who watch a game bird fly away. And they probably did.

Of the 20,000 live ducks and geese X-rayed by Dr. William H. Elder, 4 out of every 10 carried gunshot wounds.

Rock group. Amber, a hard yellow substance that seeps from trees, can trap insects. It allows scientists to have a firsthand view of life millions of years ago.

On a well-run chicken farm 1 human worker can care for 20,000 hens.

When scientists at the University of California wanted to find out the value of jogging, they turned to pigs.

In several important ways pigs are like humans. Their hearts are similar and about equal in proportion to body weight.

Besides, the eating habits of pigs and men are much alike.

Pigs, by the way, can cover a mile in 7.5 minutes running at top speed.

Cuckoo birds cuckoo 42 times a minute during the mating season, which lasts about a month.

Turkeys are so stupid they don't know enough to get out of the rain. They often catch pneumonia because they can't find the door to the poultry house. Kerchoo!

Fly bite nights: Bats may be man's best friend in keeping down mosquito bites. One bat eats about 633 mosquitoes every day, as well as large numbers of moths and beetles.

So unless you have mosquitoes, moths, and beetles around the place, don't try to housebreak a bat. You can't buy bat chow at the supermarket.

If you want to sneak up on a bird, you'll have to be triplets. Most birds can see in 2 directions at the same time. Their eyes turn separately.

A flea lives 2.5 years.

The only way to have house guests. . . .
Villagers in Equador have an understanding with South America's dread army ants, which feed on insects.

Families move out when the ants move in. After the ants leave, the people return to vacuum-clean homes.

Cats eat a third of the canned fish in America.

When the United States passed a law against selling weapons to South Africa, it ended the private war between a bird lover and neighborhood cats.

Llewellyn Clark of Knysna, South Africa, had bought a small catapult from a California manufacturer. He used it to fire mud balls at the backsides of cats hunting in his bird sanctuary.

When parts wore out, Clark ordered new ones from California. But the company wouldn't deliver because of the arms ban.

The largest winged creature that has ever flown soared the skies of West Texas 60 million years ago.

Called *Texas pterosaur*, its wings spread more than 50 feet—8 feet more than the wingspan of the United States Air Force F-15 Eagle fighter plane and almost 6 times that of the American condor, the largest flying bird now on earth.

The huge creature was a member of the pterodactyl family of reptiles. Unlike its small cousins, it did not skim the surface of the oceans and lakes searching for fish. It was a meat eater. Scientists believe it fed on dead dinosaurs.

In a race from France to northwest England on July 9, 1977, a young racing pigeon named Salty got lost. Bravely he kept going—2,400 miles across the Atlantic to safety aboard a ship near the coast of Canada. He was flown home by jet.

Flaky news: If your gerbils have dandruff, look out. You might catch a brand new disease—gerbil-keeper's lung. It can give you fever and cause difficulty in breathing.

Luckily there is an easy cure. Wear a mask over your nose and mouth when cleaning your gerbil's cage. And air out the room.

The first white lions known to exist—3 cubs—were sighted in South Africa in 1975.

Unlike albinos, which simply lack color, the lions have normal brown noses and yellow eyes. They may be the start of a new strain.

Up in Lewiston, Maine, a pet shop owner uses dogs to foretell whether the country is in for good times or bad.

Small dogs are bought when people feel they can afford a luxury, according to Sheldon Segall. Big dogs are for when people feel low and need protection.

If people start buying small dogs, good times are ahead, he says. A move to big dogs spells bad news.

Some 1,000 different kinds of wildlife creatures are threatened with extinction. More than 100 are native to the United States.

Does your dad moan about losing money in the stock market?

Take heed. Anthony Silverman of Minneapolis, Minnesota, claims to have discovered a way to choose winning stocks.

He lays the newspaper pages with the stock listings on his office floor. Then he lets his dog walk on them.

Wherever the first nail on her right paw touches, that's the stock he buys. The dog's performance, he says, has been "miraculous."

More than a century after the death of the Pony Express, America is down to one horseback mailman.

Thirteen days a month Lloyd Parson picks up mail at the tiny post office in Avent, West Virginia. He carries it on a 17-mile route to 30 houses.

Summers he drives a Jeep. He turns to his mare Ginger from November through May, when knee-deep snow can clog the dirt roads.

"Been riding horses since I was in diapers," he said in 1978. "Don't ever intend to stop."

Record Breakers

Why do people row across the Atlantic Ocean, or walk on their hands for nearly 900 miles?

Because records are made to be broken.

Even if you don't have a rowboat, or you get dizzy just standing on your head, you can set a record. Do something longer, faster, higher, or bigger.

Or dream up a stunt that has never been tried before.

Here are the records set by boys and girls in 1977 —a record year for setting records.

Two 17-year-olds, Matt Gonzalez and Pia Anderson, broke the world's playground swinging record. They began swinging in the Victor Elementary School playground in Torrance, California, on December 16, and didn't stop for 182 hours.

Students at Miraleste High School in Palos Verdes Peninsula, California, take world records seriously. They hold at least 3.

In 1976 a total of 1,468 students and teachers sat on each other's laps without a chair in a circle on the football field. Some records were broken, but no one knows exactly how many or what for.

The second record was clearer. Two juniors rode swings nonstop for 125 hours. The record lasted less than a year.

For homecoming in 1977, the 1,582 students brought pull-tops from metal cans to school for a month. They finished hooking 30,336 tops together on November 4, in time to stretch them around the football field at halftime.

The 2,169-foot necklace of pull-tops nearly circled the field twice.

It's probably another world record. But a fellow can't be sure.

The only other pull-top chain worth mentioning was made by 5 Port Huron, Michigan, schoolboys in April, 6 months earlier. It had 6,000 tabs and measured 500 feet.

Lyndon Hart, 16, of Watertown, South Dakota, swallowed 501 live goldfish as a crowd of 300 cheered him during his town's Crazy Days.

Standing beside a tank containing 1,000 goldfish,

Lyndon gulped for 3 hours 11 minutes on August 6. After only 2 hours 22 minutes he had polished off fish number 401. It shattered the record of a California youth who had eaten 400 goldfish in 5.5 hours.

"I feel great," Lyndon announced after his record meal, and promptly topped it off with a glass of soda pop and a hot dog.

Give kids enough rope, and . . . .

It began with the cold weather. Louis P. Daniels, principal of St. Victor's School in Monroe, Wisconsin, cast about for a way his students could exercise indoors.

He hit upon rope jumping, which did not need costly new equipment.

From there the kids took over.

Thirty-eight of them jumped 8 turns on a 100-foot rope in the gym on February 4. That broke the record set in 1975 by 35 kids in Lorain, Ohio.

On February 11, a week later, 44 jumpers did 5 turns.

Then a Colorado school claimed 51 jumpers.

St. Victor's came back. Fifty-two boys and girls jumped 4 turns of the 100-foot rope on May 1.

Aaron Wenzel of Dubuque, Iowa, started collecting used bus tickets at the age of 9. By 1977, when he was 13, he had 40,400.

If his record seems untouchable, take heart. Aaron

has announced his retirement. The tickets will be recycled.

A class of seventh graders at Nazareth Area Junior High School in Pennsylvania formed a chain of clovers 800 feet long in June.

Two New York girls, Meryl Brodsky, 14, of Coram, and Barbara Clanton, 15, of Seldon, wove together 5 pounds of chewing-gum wrappers into a chain 314 feet long. The old record was a gummy 198 feet.

The girls joined forces in October after discovering they were working on chains separately. They shared the work, but did not say who did the chewing.

The age-group champ of beer can collectors is Kenneth J. Wilson, Jr., 14, of Boardman, Ohio.

By 1977 he had been collecting for only 2 years. Yet he had filled the basement shelves of his home with 1,400 different brands of empty cans from around the world.

One of his prized cans is labeled "Tivoli." That's "I-lov-it" spelled backwards.

What about sore throats and accidents?

"I had them on weekends," said Steven Ladd, who

never missed a day of school from the first grade through high school.

Steven, 16, finished those 2,160 days, spread over 12 years, as valedictorian at Maynard Evans High School in Orlando, Florida.

But alas, there are more school days in Michigan than in Florida. And so *pfft!* went Steven Ladd's record.

Walter J. Gorski of St. Mary's High School in Royal Oak, Michigan, took the crown. He had a perfect attendance of 2,184 days—24 more than Steven.

Walter gave credit to his trusty alarm clock.

Junior Mamoe, 11, of San Francisco, California, saw the movie *Rocky* 77 times in 1977. He planned to keep seeing it as long as he could.

One theater manager let Junior in free after he'd seen the picture 50 times.

The theater made enough money on Junior at the food stand. One day he downed a hot dog, 3 soft drinks, 3 chocolate sundaes, some candy, and a box of popcorn.

Bravo for Patty Wilson, 15, an epileptic. She set an unofficial women's world record by jogging the 1,350 miles from her home in La Palma, California, to Portland, Oregon. She wanted to prove that epileptics can lead normal and active lives.

Patty started running early each morning and quit about 4 P.M. each evening. She averaged 40 miles a day. The 42-day run ended July 29.

Oregon's governor, Bob Straub, left his office to jog the last mile with her.

Building a house is as good a way as any to pass a slow Sunday. In June the 3 Yurkanin brothers—

Bryan, 13; Mark, 11; and Matthew, 6—thought so.

They built a 6-story house out of 2,200 playing, trading, and game cards.

Their shaky high-rise easily topped the old record. A 2-story 2,000-card house had been built only a week earlier by 5 boys in Kenmore, New York.

The 3 brothers didn't sneeze, cough, or breathe too deeply during the 5 hours of piling cards on the floor of their home in Hazleton, Pennsylvania.

They hope to keep adding to the house—if they find more cards.

Winner by an eyelash is Carolyn Peterson, 15, of Bloomfield Hills, Michigan.

A lash above her right eye measures 1¾ inches. It's the longest seen so far.

The tip is dark, like the others. The rest of the lash, about 1½ inches, is white and curls down onto her cheek.

Mike Kleeman, 17, of Bremerton, Washington, crawled 9.2 miles to break the old world record of 9 miles set by a Seattle man.

Mike started his knee-skinner on October 17. He finished 21 hours later. The feat raised $625 for

North Kitsap High School's "Save Our Activities Program."

Mike hoped to crawl farther, but his mother made him come home.

Beth Boyle and Mary Murphy, both 13, of Port Richmond, New York, rested their ears August 27. They had listened for 72 straight hours to the records of the Beatles, an English rock group of the 1960s.

Were they fed up?

"No," said Beth's mother. "They are just as enthusiastic about the Beatles as they were before they started."

David W. Horton, 16, pedaled a 1-wheeler 85 miles in 11 hours 15 minutes. He beat the 85-mile

unicycle record of 14 hours 35 minutes by a bouncing 3 hours 20 minutes.

Because he took several allowed stops, his actual riding time was 10 hours 24 minutes. His average speed was a nifty 8.2 miles per hour.

David had planned to pedal 95 miles when he started out. He was still thinking about it when cramps struck halfway through the return trip to Lakehurst, New Jersey, where he lives.

The pain hit both knees and the insides of his thighs.

"If I concentrated real hard," he said, "I could put the pain out of my mind for a few minutes at a time."

You can't coast on a 1-wheeler. You have to pedal every second.

David biked from 6 A.M. until 5:15 P.M. He braved August heat of 83 degrees, occasional showers, and winds up to 20 miles per hour. He sweated off 5 pounds.

The rain was a blessing of sorts. It refreshed him. But his father had to keep drying off his eyeglasses.

"I had to watch out for potholes," said David. His only fall came when he hit a pothole hidden by a puddle.

Would he do it again?

"I suppose I'd consider trying to break whatever new record was set," he said. "But I'm not going to get sick over it."

Ninety students at Springville Junior High School in Utah went to bed one night in May, thoroughly punchy. With good reason.

They had punched out 225,000 staples in making a paper chain of more than 15 miles.

The boys and girls spent 5.5 hours at the task. They cut newspapers into 2-inch-wide strips, formed loops, and stapled them together into a chain 81,148 feet long.

There were enough sections left to add another 5 miles.

But 15 miles were enough to outstrip the paper

chain record of 14 miles set the month before by 30 students at the Beth Sholom Synagogue in Cheltenham, Pennsylvania.

No one bothered to claim a staple-punching record.

How does liver go down? Not easily, according to Bill Lee, 16, of Payson High School in Payson, Arizona.

Nevertheless, Bill ate his way to glory by downing 2 pounds in 15.5 minutes. The meat had been cut into narrow strips, and he mistakenly tried to chew the first piece. No luck. He gagged, and tears streamed down his face.

Instantly the owner of the pickup truck in which Bill was standing bellowed, "Don't throw up in my truck!"

Friends among the 40 onlookers shouted encouragement. "Slow down." "Take your time." "Don't try to chew it."

Bill slid the other strips down his throat without chewing. Besides the record, he earned $120 in pledges for his sophomore class treasury.

Two teen-age girls set the world's record for continuous card playing.

Kim Baker, 14, and Susan McGann, 13, both of Silver Springs, Florida, started playing at 9:15 A.M. on July 12 and didn't quit until 1:25 A.M., July 16 —88 hours and 10 minutes later.

The girls played in an all-night restaurant where they were observed around the clock. They did not sleep and took only a 5-minute break each hour.

They wore out two decks of cards playing rummy, blackjack, go fish, and war. When they ran out of games, they invented their own. Occasionally passersby would stop and chat with them and teach them new games.

"Near the last couple of hours I started hallucinating," said Kim. "That was when we decided we had better stop. The next day it was hard to remember all that had happened."

Two New York high school boys, Eugene McDevitt, 16, of Rexford, and John Krauss, 17, of Niskayuna, began curling on Christmas Day. They took only a 5-minute rest period every hour.

For 15 hours and 25 minutes they slid the 40-pound stones back and forth over the 146-foot curling sheet 1,328 times, for a total of 53,120 pounds, bettering the old mark by an hour and 2 seconds and 4,720 pounds.

Body English

If you want to know how big your heart is, look at your fist. They are about the same size, and they grow at about the same rate.

A computer that could do all the things a human brain can do would have to be housed in the biggest building in the world.

More people are killed by accidentally choking on food than by guns, airplane accidents, electrical shock, or lightning.

The colder the room you sleep in, the better are your chances of having a bad dream.

You breathe about 10 million times a year.

Coughs and sneezes spread diseases. But if you hold back a sneeze, you can break a muscle in your face, or cause a nosebleed or even a stroke.

Three out of 4 Americans saw a doctor in 1976.

A study in England found that grown-ups whose last names begin with the letters from S to Z are twice as likely as others to get ulcers and 3 times as likely to have heart attacks.

Now hear this. A decibel is a unit for measuring loudness.

If you listen to a rock band live and close up, you may be inviting deafness. Hearing is harmed by noises above 115 decibels. Many rock groups hit 150 to 160 decibels, louder than a jet airplane taking off.

Most fat babies grow up to become fat adults.

One half of all visits to the school nurse are made by the same 15 percent of students.

You could be in serious danger if you haven't had shots against 7 serious diseases.

The Public Health Service says that almost 4 out

HAROLD TRIES TO PUT THINGS OFF AS LONG AS POSSIBLE.

of every 10 kids under 15 have never had shots against tetanus, whooping cough, polio, red measles, German measles, mumps, and diphtheria.

The bumps on your tongue hold about 9,000 taste buds.

Chin up! If you don't want a double chin, avoid sleeping on a high pillow.

In the Youth Fitness Test, given to millions of kids since 1965, girls improve until the age of 13 or 14. Then their scores level off. Boys' scores keep rising as they grow older.

The average man's brain weighs 49 ounces. The average woman's brain weighs 44 ounces. However, there is no proof yet that the weight of the brain has anything to do with how smart you are.

A cubic inch of bone will withstand 2 tons. That's double the strength of oak.

Itchy witchy. There are more creatures such as mites, yeast, and bacteria living on your skin than there are people living on earth.

Guide to fingernail biters.
Fingernails grow faster on the right hand of right-handed persons, faster on the left hand of left-handed persons.
Fingernails grow a fifth faster in summer than in winter, and twice as fast during the day as at night.
The middle fingernail grows fastest.

The heart and not the brain was once believed to be the center of learning. Thus the old saying: "To learn by heart."

The skin of a newly born baby is usually wrinkled because it is too big. It may take 6 months for a baby's body to fill out.

Why knuckles crack: When you pull apart the 2 bones of your finger joint, a fluid slips into the space. This results in a low-pressure condition, which in turn causes bubbles to form and then collapse. The collapse is the "cracking" sound.

The lung is the only organ that does what it does without using any energy. Air is pulled in and pushed out by the muscles of the diaphragm and chest.

Your hair is as strong as aluminum.

About 20 million Americans don't have a tooth in their heads.

Aspirin Alley

Many, many books have been written about people who have done great or evil deeds, or who are simply rich, good-looking, or lucky.

Nowhere has the proper attention been given to the underdog, the bonehead, the innocent victim, the unlucky Harry. His moment of fame has too long been overlooked.

To make up for such neglect, Aspirin Alley welcomes:

—Joe Hayden, 17, who issued a challenge to play chess with 180 people at one time.

Unfortunately 20 people showed up in a shopping center in Cardiff, New Jersey, in August, 1977, to accept the challenge. Eighteen defeated him, including a 7-year-old boy, Stowell Fulton.

Joe beat only his mother and a man who quit early to go shopping.

—Mr. and Mrs. Robert Ghattas of Albuquerque, New Mexico, whose son Marco, 11, went over their heads in 1977.

Marco wrote to Governor Jerry Apodaca, a friend of the family. His letter asked the governor to drop a note to his parents giving him permission to eat in the TV room. He got the letter—and permission.

—The Lucas brothers, Mark, 10, and Paul, 8, of Fairfield, Connecticut, who got one less Christmas present in 1977.

Police blasted apart their Christmas package with a shotgun after spotting several wires inside it by means of X ray. The package held clothes and walkie-talkies.

—Ben Rogers Lee, a champion wild turkey caller, who likes to keep in shape.

In January, 1978, he went out to the woods near Coffeeville, Alabama, to practice his turkey calls. He was so good that he got hit with 16 buckshot from the gun of a turkey hunter.

—Rosendo Cruz of Alhambra, California, whose stolen car seemed to have gone underground, so completely did it disappear. Police didn't unearth it for 3 years.

In February, 1978, two officers were flagged down by children who had been digging in their backyard. The officers, aided by a heavy crane, pulled out Cruz's green Ferrari. The car was worth at least $18,000 when it was purchased new in 1974.

Cruz had reported it stolen 4 months after buying it. It was found in good condition. But no one knows why it was buried, or by whom.

—Aliahu Aziz of Tel Aviv, Israel, who wanted to plant an avocado tree in his garden in honor of his daughter's third birthday in December, 1977.

After a little digging, he uncovered a live mortar shell. The more he dug, the more shells he uncovered.

Aziz and his family had been living 12 years over a World War I ammunition dump.

—Bobby Fields, 13, who in December, 1977, was biking in a parking lot in Salem, Oregon, and found a check for $10,000. It had slipped from the pocket of Elmer Stoller.

Stoller gave Bobby a reward—$2.00.

—Doug Pritchard, 13, of Tulenoir, North Carolina, who went to the doctor in January, 1978, because his foot hurt.

There was, he learned, a tooth growing out of it. "A rare case of 'genetic misdirection,'" said the doctor, and yanked out the lonely chopper.

—Edward Bruening of Cleveland, Ohio, who in 1977 got into a tickling bout with his son Jamie, a 17-month-old "little angel" with a devilishly quick

right. Bruening ended up with his jaw wired shut for 6 weeks.

—King James I of England, who planted a black mulberry tree at Buckingham Palace in 1607.

The king hoped to encourage landowners to buy and plant 10,000 mulberries and make London the center of the European silk trade.

Somebody forgot to tell him that silkworms prefer the leaves of the *white* mulberry.

—Mike Maryn, 56, of Passaic, New Jersey, who was mugged 83 times between 1973 and 1977. Police offered him a walkie-talkie so he could summon help.

"No thanks," he said. "It would only be stolen from me."

—The government clerk in Australia who made a slight error in his paperwork.

As a result a $300,000 police headquarters was built in St. Arnaud's (population 3,000) instead of in St. Alban's (population 40,000) in 1977.

Part of the new construction is a 50-car parking lot. It is used by the 2 cars and 2 bicycles of the St. Arnaud's police department.

—The Tennessee Valley Authority, which had to close its nuclear power plant at Knoxville on September 18, 1977. Reason: a worker's overshoe fell into an atomic reactor. The plant stayed closed for 17 days, at a cost of $2.8 million.

—Mrs. J. L. Butler of Alexandria, Louisiana, who removed the name bracelets from her newborn twin daughters as a joke to confuse her husband—and became confused herself.

To find out who was who, she took Amanda Mae

and Miranda Kae, born November 2, 1977, back to the hospital. Officials there had to call in the sheriff's office to solve the case.

THAT'S GREAT, HONEY. NOW, WHICH ONE IS WHICH?

—Mrs. Georgia Brauer of Santa Cruz, California, who felt the heavy hand of justice when she reported for jury duty in January, 1978. The judge was her husband, Harry.

"You can't serve on a jury in this court," he told her. "You don't pay any attention to anything I say at home. There is no reason to believe you would listen to anything I say here."

He sent her to another courtroom.

—Phillip Brown, who changed jobs after working 17 years for the Royal Society for the Protection of Birds. In 1966 he became editor of *Shooting Times*, an English hunting magazine.

—The Wedgewood Health Care Center, a nursing home in Inver Grove Heights, Minnesota, which got soaked by its water bill.

Edward Lehmann, in charge of the home, tried saving water. He sent out the laundry. He let the lawns go unsprinkled.

Still the water bill climbed.

After 3 years of complaining, he finally got inspectors to come and take a look in February, 1978.

The inspectors discovered what was wrong. The water meter had been put in backwards.

Lehmann received a check for $19,812 in payment of overcharges.

—Jean Smith, who moved into an apartment in Belmont, California, in January, 1978. When she opened the dishwasher, she saw a 7-foot-long boa constrictor staring back at her.

The snake had been left behind by the former

occupant, Laura Ramstetter, a dancer, who used it in her act. She thought it had escaped from the apartment.

The snake's name: Huggy.

—The runners in the Boston Marathon of 1907, who got railroaded by winner Tom Longboat.

An Onondaga Indian from Ontario, Canada, Longboat reached a track-crossing first and sprinted across it ahead of an oncoming train. His rivals were left to wait for the mile of freight cars to pass.

—The people of Sweden, who in 1659 had to lug around a new issue of metal coins.

Each coin weighed 38.5 pounds, the heaviest in history.

—William Shakespeare, the great English playwright, who goofed on his dates. In his comedy *Troilus and Cressida* he has a character in the Trojan War talk about Aristotle, who was not born until centuries later.

—Don Wilson, 16, of Gillingham, England, who rescued his dog from a pond in November, 1977. Don's reward: a bite on his finger that required 5 stitches.

—The thieves who stole the wrong truck from a city parking lot in Brockton, Massachusetts, in January, 1978.

Quite obviously they had meant to steal the truck parked alongside. It was loaded with drugs, razor blades, and tools.

Instead they made off with a truck filled with 4.5 tons of fire hydrants and 2 tons of a booklet titled *Toilet Training for Children*.

—Jerri Morgan, who had to prizefight as part of her police training program in Columbus, Ohio.

That's why she found herself in the ring with a man, fellow cadet John Todhunter.

"Put yourself in my shoes," said Todhunter afterward. "I hit her a little to let her know what it feels like."

Recovering with an ice bag, Ms. Morgan said, "I tried to keep my eyes on him, but all I could see was this big glove."

—Students at Miami Jackson High School in Miami, Florida, who had to look at their grades.

In the 1977 statewide skills test, 78 percent flunked the math half and 27 percent flunked the communications half.

—Dan Cameron Rodill, 37, who jumped from the Brooklyn Bridge in New York City on August 29, 1977.

He wanted to call attention to his playwriting. He got 13 broken ribs for his stunt, but no calls from producers.

—The 30 students who returned to Emory University in Atlanta, Georgia, and found they were homeless.

While they were away over Christmas vacation in 1977, the fire alarm system in their fraternity house went haywire. It started a fire that burned the house to the ground.

—The modern art lovers and critics who in 1964 "oohed" and "aahed" over the powerful brush strokes of an unknown artist, "Pierre Brassau."

Being locked behind bars, Brassau couldn't attend the show in Göteborg, Sweden. So his oil paintings were entered by a group of smiling newspapermen.

One of his pictures sold for $90. Not a fortune, but more than "Pierre Brassau," age 4½, a West African chimpanzee, could spend in his lifetime.

—Engineers at the University of Florida, who in 1977 learned that the nuclear reactor they built must be shut down every time a toilet in the building is flushed.

—Charo, a female entertainer who is upset by unnecessary names and years. She went to court in 1977 to have her *age* changed—from 36 to 26.

—The people who live along a 1-mile stretch of road in Tampa, Florida. They complained that motorists ignored the speed limit of 30 miles per hour.

The city fathers acted. On January 2, 1978, they raised the speed limit to 35 miles per hour.

—Pete Pickett, who in 1963 put on fake gorilla feet and tramped over his favorite squirrel-hunting ground in Coosa Valley, Alabama.

He hoped the footprints would scare away other squirrel hunters. Instead the footprints drew mobs of Big Foot hunters.

—Superheavyweight William H. Taft, who got stuck in his White House bathtub.

He replaced the bathtub with a bigger one. An extra big one. His weight while he was President see-sawed between 265 and 332 pounds.

—The American automobile makers who in 1977 had to recall a record 12.6 million motor vehicles because of problems affecting safety.

And let's not forget Gerico, Inc., a company that makes baby strollers in Boulder, Colorado. It had to recall 40,000 strollers in 1977. A poorly made lock could cause the stroller to fold inward while in use.

—Pedro Juan Vinales of Puerto Rico, a jockey who retired in 1961 at the early age of 28. He had ridden in 360 races and won 0.

—The St. Louis, Missouri, fire department, whose headquarters were found to be a fire hazard.

Fire inspector Raymond Hammond, who inspected the 3-story building in October, 1977, said none of the violations of 5 years earlier had been corrected.

—Editors of the Portland, Oregon, Community College catalogue, who had a little trouble themselves in writing up 4 grammar courses. They spelled it *grammer*.

—The thief who tried to enter a house in Houston, Texas, by the chimney 3 days before Christmas, 1977. Not being Santa Claus exactly, he became stuck.

He had no plans to try again.

—Skip Swenson of Los Angeles, California, who chose the word *NONE* for his license plate instead of numbers in 1977.

Next thing he knew, he was socked with a bill for $953 worth of unpaid parking tickets.

Seems the police of Reno, Nevada, where Swenson works, write the word *NONE* on a parking ticket whenever they see a car with no license plate. The computer did the rest.

—Ted Simmonds, who said, "I'll try to move a bit more."

In 1961 Ted, 12, was goalie for an English soccer team called the Workshop Sea Cadets. During the first 8 games he let in 204 goals.

With such leaky goaltending, his team was sunk by scores of 25–1, 33–0, 28–0, 34–0, 34–0, 11–3, 25–1, and 14–0.

—Thomas Helms, 27, a down-on-his-luck artist who tried to end it all just before Christmas, 1977.

He jumped from the eighty-sixth floor of the Empire State Building in New York City. Someone higher up liked him, because a 30-mile-per-hour wind blew him unharmed onto a ledge a floor below.

—Jerry and Darlene Jenkins of Burlington, Vermont. While they were honeymooning in New York City, their car was seized at gunpoint on December 4, 1977. The couple was taken for a reckless ride that injured 15 persons.

Mayor Abe Beame apologized. "We're sorry this

happened," he said, and loaded the honeymooners down with gifts.

Everything was dandy till a hometown merchant saw Jerry's picture in the newspapers. On December 9, Jerry was arrested on charges of cashing more than $2,500 worth of bad checks in Vermont stores.

—Bill Stanton of Chicago, Illinois, who on November 21, 1977, found a skunk in his garage and watched his troubles grow.

After no city department would help him get it out, he bought a trap and discovered he'd unlawfully done the following: (1) brought a trap into the city; (2) trapped in the city; (3) trapped without a license.

Worse, he learned that it is unlawful to keep a skunk, to destroy it, or to let it go free, because it might carry diseases.

—Tamara Torbert, 15, who ended up a sore loser in a 1977 battle with the Mesquite, Texas, school board.

Her mother protested when Tamara was paddled for constantly being late. When the school board wouldn't back down, Mrs. Torbert agreed to paddle Tamara herself—in the principal's office.

—King Edward III of England, who thought he could stamp out bowling. In 1366 he outlawed the game because it took his soldiers away from archery practice.

—Henry Wells, driver of a Duryea Motor Wagon, who struck bicyclist Evylyn Thomas on a New York City street on May 30, 1896, causing the first automobile accident.

—Harry Caldwell, chief of police of Houston, Texas, who in 1977 was doing pretty well in front of 180 kindergarten and first grade pupils.

Then a boy raised his hand and asked, "How come you haven't found my bicycle?"

"He just didn't understand my manpower shortage," said the chief.

—Fred Brown, who in November, 1963, was named "Florida Lineman of the Week" for his game against Purdue.

His football coaches at the University of Miami blinked. After viewing films of the game, they had demoted Brown to the second team.

—Six rooters of Maine's Livermore Falls High School basketball team, who in 1965 decided their school spirit needed a lift.

Hoping to set an example, they dribbled 2 basketballs the 22 miles to Farmington, where the team was to play.

Neither Maine's December winds nor freezing rain stopped them. Wet, tired, chilled, but full of spirit, they reached the gym—the empty gym.

The game had been postponed owing to dangerous road conditions.

—Robert LaCarte of Escanaba, Michigan, who chose the wrong day in January, 1978—Friday the 13th—to do a bit of quiet ice fishing.

LaCarte drove his snowmobile to his shack on frozen Lake Michigan. When he emerged after dark, he saw the snowmobile floating off on an island of ice. Another thing: He was surrounded by water.

A helicopter rescued him after two snowmobilers saw his signal—the fire that burned down his shack.

—Brenda Sublett, 22, of Lakeland, Florida, who climbed a tree to pick mistletoe for the 1977 holidays. She got stuck and had to be rescued by firemen with a chain saw.

—Ray Valine, who went back to California after failing to earn a living as a human billboard.

Merchants in Baton Rouge, Louisiana, weren't willing to pay $300 to $500 a day to advertise on his shaved head during Super Bowl week, 1978.

—Julie Dulduao, 16, who had the shortest reign of any beauty queen.

Crowned winner of the 1977 Miss Philippines–USA beauty contest, she was told the next day she had been dethroned. The judges had goofed the ballot count.

The real winner was runner-up Rosemary Englar, 17.

—A Pinellas County teacher's union. It flunked its effort to get the Florida legislature to keep the office of commissioner of education in 1978.

The union sent telegrams to "chairman" Louis de la Parte. He wasn't even on the commission. The telegrams also called Robert Shevin "lieutenant governor." He was the attorney general.

—Terry Trent, who learned how carefully his *Shoppers News* is read.

Each Wednesday the free weekly advertising newspaper in Little Rock, Arkansas, ran a lucky number sweepstakes. Readers were pleased—especially after an edition in February, 1978.

The lucky number was 69161, worth $250. Thousands of men and women telephoned and jammed the roads to the newspaper's office. They *all* claimed the cash prize.

Trent blamed a mechanical error. Every copy—every single one of the 39,000—had printed the same number, 69161.

The money went to Paul Staggs, the first to call in.

And a final fact for young sleuths. Don't try to hide if you have on squeaky sneakers.

BROOKDALE